DOGBERT'S

CLUES FOR THE CLUELESS

Scott Adams

DO WE HAVE ANY CLUELESS PEOPLE HERE TODAY ?

Andrews and McMeel
A Universal Press Syndicate Company
Kansas City

To Sarah and Freddie and Freddie's Mom

Library of Congress Catalog Card Number: 93-71864

ISBN: 0-8362-1737-3

First Printing, July 1993
Twelfth Printing, December 1996

CONTENTS

Many years ago, a group of mischievous cave people were sitting in their little cave dwelling, chewing on dinosaur parts and thinking up cruel tricks to play on future generations. They decided it would be a major hoot to invent a whole bunch of inconvenient behaviors, teach them to their children and act as if it all made perfect sense.

Their plan was that when the children became adults — at about age six in those days — the elders would reveal their little joke, then roll around in their rancid fur loincloths, laughing until they got brain damage. Remember, this was before alcohol or cigarettes were invented. They were just being resourceful.

Anyway, before the adults could own up to their cruel hoax, they were all crushed by a stampede of frightened woolly mammoths who had accidentally walked across a carpet, thus generating the biggest wad of static electricity ever seen at that time. (You see, they were very woolly.)

So the children grew up never knowing that the moronic behaviors they learned from their parents were meant as a big joke. These behaviors were passed down from generation to generation, eventually being labeled "etiquette" because it sounds French, which makes sense for reasons I won't go into.

But lots of things have changed in the millions of years since etiquette was invented. Microwave ovens, for example. And so it seemed like a good time to update the rules of etiquette. That's why I wrote this book.

Of course, you could buy some other book on etiquette, and in it you might find such useful tidbits as what kind of uniform the upstairs servants should wear, or the proper way to address the Pope when you meet him in person. But if you want practical information — like what to do after you sneeze in your hand — then you have to buy this book. It's the only book that speaks to you as the unwashed heathen that you know you are.

Thanks. And I'm not just saying that.

Dogbert

EATING AND DRINKING

THERE IS NO GOOD REASON TO WAIT FOR OTHER PEOPLE TO BE SERVED BEFORE YOU START EATING.

UNDER TRADITIONAL RULES OF ETIQUETTE EVERYBODY SITS AWKWARDLY UNTIL THE LAST PERSON IS SERVED.

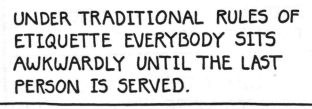

YOUR SOUP WILL BE READY IN FEBRUARY.

THE DOGBERT METHOD TOTALLY ELIMINATES THE AWKWARD AND UNNECESSARY WAITING PERIOD.

EATING OFF SOMEBODY ELSE'S PLATE

DOGBERT'S CLUES FOR THE CLUELESS

RESTAURANTS AND SCREAMING KIDS

CHILDREN ARE EXEMPT FROM ETIQUETTE IN RESTAURANTS AND SO ARE THEIR PARENTS.

IT IS ACCEPTED PRACTICE TO BRING YOUR SCREAMING CHILD INTO FINE RESTAURANTS AND IGNORE HIM.

AAAAAAH!

IT IS NOT ACCEPTABLE TO USE YOUR TABLE BREAD TO MUFFLE THE NOISE.

WAITER, WE NEED MORE BREAD.

YOUR BEST BET IS TO BE DIRECT BUT BE GRACIOUS.

CHAMPAGNE AND A VASECTOMY, COMPLIMENTS OF TABLE THREE.

DRINKING FROM THE CONTAINER

TIPPING THE WAITER

HERE ARE SOME TIPS ON TIPPING THAT YOU WON'T GET ANYWHERE ELSE.

IF THE SERVICE IS PROMPT BUT THE WAITER IS OBNOXIOUS, TOSS THE TIP ON THE FLOOR AND MAKE HIM CRAWL.

PENALIZE THE WAITER FOR POOR FOOD QUALITY OR ANYTHING ELSE THAT'S BOTHERING YOU LATELY.

MINUS A DOLLAR BECAUSE PEOPLE TAILGATE.

TIP IN ADVANCE IF YOU HAVE ANY SPECIAL REQUESTS.

HERE'S A BUCK. STOP MAKING CLEVER CONVERSATION WITH US.

VEGETARIAN ETIQUETTE

WATER FOUNTAINS

IT IS RUDE TO TOUCH A PUBLIC WATER FOUNTAIN WITH YOUR LIPS, UNLESS YOU HAVE DEVELOPED A RELATIONSHIP WITH IT.

S. Adams

RUDE

SLURP GURGLE

VERY RUDE!

SLURP GURGLE

CORRECT

ALTHOUGH I HAVEN'T KNOWN YOU LONG, ALREADY I'M THIRSTY.

WHEN WOMEN PAY FOR DINNER

MANY MEN ARE STILL UNCOMFORTABLE WHEN A WOMAN INSISTS ON PICKING UP THE CHECK. FOR THE MAN, THERE IS ONLY ONE CORRECT RESPONSE.

WRONG*: HITTING HER WITH THE BUTT OF YOUR GUN.

* EXCEPT IN UTAH

WRONG: TRYING HUMOR TO LIGHTEN THE TENSION.

NOW I GUESS I'LL HAVE TO SLEEP WITH YOU! HAW HAW!

CORRECT: RETURN TO THE OCEAN LIKE THE JELLYFISH YOU'VE BECOME.

S. Adams

EMPLOYEE EGOS

IT IS BAD FORM TO DISCUSS YOUR SUPERIOR LIFE IN FRONT OF LOWER LEVEL EMPLOYEES.

S. Adams

DON'T TALK ABOUT YOUR INCOME.

ALL I DID WAS WALK AROUND TODAY... AND I MADE TWICE YOUR SALARY.

DON'T TALK ABOUT THEIR CUBICLES.

THIS CUBICLE REMINDS ME OF THE CARDBOARD BOX THAT MY BIG SCREEN TV CAME IN.

DON'T TALK ABOUT YOUR ACCESS TO A MORE BOUNTIFUL SEX LIFE.

I THINK I'LL GO USE MY POSITION OF POWER AS AN APHRODISIAC.

BEING LATE FOR MEETINGS

THE ACCEPTABLE LEVEL OF LATENESS FOR A MEETING DEPENDS ON WHAT YOU THINK OF THE OTHER ATTENDEES.

YOU CAN BE SEVEN MINUTES LATE FOR A MEETING WITH CO-WORKERS FOR WHOM YOU HAVE NO REAL RESPECT.

I WAS DOING MY MAIL.

S. Adams

YOU CAN BE FIFTEEN MINUTES LATE FOR A MEETING WITH PEOPLE WHO ARE — IN YOUR OPINION — FETID PILES OF GARBAGE.

I FORGOT TO LOOK AT MY CALENDAR.

IF YOU'RE AN IMPORTANT EXECUTIVE YOU CAN BE AN HOUR LATE, BECAUSE TO YOU ALL THE EMPLOYEES LOOK LIKE FETID GARBAGE WITH BAD ATTITUDES.

I'D TELL YOU WHY I'M LATE BUT YOU WOULDN'T UNDERSTAND

ELEVATOR EFFICIENCY

POLITE BEHAVIOR IN ELEVATORS CAN SERIOUSLY IMPACT YOUR SCHEDULE. USE THESE TRICKS TO BE MORE EFFICIENT.

SCOWL AT THOSE WHO TAKE THE ELEVATOR FOR ONE FLOOR; IT MAY REDUCE FUTURE ABUSES.

STAND DIRECTLY IN FRONT OF THE ELEVATOR AS THOUGH YOU ARE THE ONLY PERSON ON EARTH.

YOU DON'T HAVE TO HOLD THE ELEVATOR IF YOU PRETEND YOU DON'T SEE ANYBODY COMING.

S. Adams

ELEVATOR ETIQUETTE

THERE ARE SOME THINGS YOU SHOULD NEVER DO ON AN ELEVATOR.

NEVER FACE THE BACK. IT MAKES PEOPLE NERVOUS.

NEVER STAND NEXT TO A PERSON IF THERE ARE ONLY TWO OF YOU.

DON'T TRY TO CRUSH PEOPLE BY PUSHING THE "CLOSE" BUTTON. I'VE TRIED IT AND IT DOESN'T WORK.

CLOSE

MY SECRETARY THE BOSS

YOU MAY DEBASE YOUR SECRETARY BY WHIMSIC- ALLY REFERRING TO HIM OR HER AS YOUR "BOSS."

S.Adams

BEFORE WE START, LET'S GO AROUND THE TABLE AND INTRODUCE OURSELVES.

I'M LARRY, AND I WORK FOR IRENE ... HEH, HEH...

HA HA

REALLY?

HOWEVER, THERE IS A DANGER THAT THIS WILL CONFUSE PEOPLE.

YES! MY HARD WORK PAID OFF AND I DIDN'T EVEN KNOW IT. GET ME SOME COFFEE, YOU POMPOUS REAR-END!

THE LAST DONUT

IT IS IMPOLITE TO TAKE THE LAST DONUT WITHOUT OFFERING IT TO OTHERS FIRST. USE THESE TRICKS TO MAKE SURE THEY DON'T TAKE IT.

YOU TAKE IT, BETH. IT'LL HELP YOU KEEP THAT RUBENESQUE FIGURE.

HOW ABOUT YOU, WALLY? WE ALL LOVE TO WATCH THE WAY YOU EAT!

LATECOMERS TO THE MEETING ARE HARDER TO CONTROL.

DIG IN, I THINK THE FLIES GOT ALL THEY WANTED ON THIS ONE.

MANNERS AND YOUR BODY

BREAST FEEDING

YAWNING

REMEMBER THESE HANDY TIPS ON YAWNING.

S. Adams

TRY THE ONE-NOSTRIL SECRET YAWN METHOD.

COVER YOUR MOUTH SO NOBODY CAN TELL THAT YOU YAWNED.

I WONDER IF HE'S YAWNING BEHIND THAT HAND.

AAAAHH!

FOR YOUR MORE VIGOROUS YAWNS, TRY NOT TO CATCH OTHER PEOPLE IN YOUR VORTEX.

OOPS

THE SOUNDS OF EATING

BAD BREATH

NUDITY

THIS IS A SENSITIVE TOPIC, SO I'LL DEAL WITH IT IN A DELICATE AND DIGNIFIED MANNER.

IT IS EQUALLY IMPOLITE FOR ANIMALS TO WEAR PANTS AS IT IS FOR PEOPLE TO BE NUDE.

SOME EXCEPTIONS INCLUDE HAIRLESS MANX CATS WHO MUST WEAR PANTS AND, IDEALLY, A PAPER BAG...

MEOW

MEN WITH HAIRY BACKS ARE REQUIRED BY GOOD ETIQUETTE TO MOVE TO TIBET AND LIVE AS YETIS.

S. Adams

NUDITY

THE CORRECT AMOUNT OF CLOTHING DEPENDS ON CUSTOM, CONTEXT, AND GOOD JUDGEMENT.

S. Adams

FOR EXAMPLE, A WELL-DRESSED MUMMY SHOULD COVER THE ENTIRE BODY.

BUT A BEACH-GOER CAN WEAR AS LITTLE AS A THONG BIKINI.

HOWEVER, A MUMMY SHOULD NEVER WEAR A BIKINI.

LOOKING GOOD...

RUDENESS WARNING SIGNS

RATHER THAN MEMORIZING THE MANY RULES OF ETIQUETTE YOU CAN USE THESE SIMPLE EARLY WARNING INDICATORS TO AVOID RUDENESS.

STOP

IF YOUR LIPS ARE EXTENDED BEYOND YOUR NOSE THEN YOU ARE ABOUT TO DO SOMETHING RUDE.

POSSIBLE SLURP IN PROGRESS.

S. Adams

IF A LOUD NOISE IS ABOUT TO COME OUT OF YOUR BODY — AND IT IS NOT LANGUAGE — THEN YOU ARE ABOUT TO BE RUDE.

POSSIBLE BURP, SNEEZE, OR WORSE.

IF YOU USE SOMETHING FOR OTHER THAN ITS INTENDED PURPOSE YOU MAY ALREADY BE RUDE.

HONK!!

PERSONAL SPACE

YOUR PERSONAL SPACE REQUIREMENTS DEPEND ON YOUR CULTURAL INFLUENCES.

IN ITALY YOU MAY GET INSIDE ANOTHER PERSON'S CLOTHES.

HI, I'M MARIO.

S. Adams

IN THE UNITED STATES YOU ARE ALLOWED JUST INSIDE THE BAD BREATH ZONE.

BAD BREATH ZONE

IN AUSTRALIA ANY DISTANCE IS TOO DANG CLOSE.

HEY! CAN WE TALK?!

HE MUST BE A TOURIST.

MEN AND WOMEN

KEEPING YOUR SEAT (FOR MEN)

OFTEN IT IS THE MAN WHO IS EXPECTED TO GIVE UP HIS SEAT ON PUBLIC TRANSPORTATION. USE THESE TRICKS TO KEEP YOURS.

S. Adams

PRETEND TO BE ASLEEP.

ACT CRAZY AND MAYBE SOME-BODY ELSE WILL MOVE.

USE PSYCHOLOGY TO INSTILL A GREATER SENSE OF GUILT IN SOMEBODY ELSE.

SO, WHAT DO YOU THINK OF THE WOMEN'S MOVEMENT?

WOMEN'S LEG HAIR

WOMEN ARE SENSITIVE WHEN THEY HAVEN'T HAD TIME TO SHAVE THEIR LEGS. BE CAREFUL.

DO NOT TRY TO MAKE THE BEST OUT OF THE SITUATION.

WE'RE OUT OF SANDPAPER, AND I NEED TO TAKE THE EDGE OFF THIS BREAD BOARD, SO I WAS THINKING...

S. Adams

DON'T NAG.

WELL, GREAT, NOW YOU'VE KILLED THE CAT.

WHEN SHE WANTS TO SPOON, TAKE IT LIKE A MAN.

HELP!! HELP!!

COMPLIMENTING A WOMAN

THE PROPER METHOD FOR COMPLIMENTING A WOMAN ON HER APPEARANCE DEPENDS ON YOUR SOCIAL AND ECONOMIC STATUS.

THE WEALTHY

I SIMPLY MUST HAVE THE NAME OF YOUR PLASTIC SURGEON.

I'M FLATTERED.

MIDDLE CLASS

THAT OUTFIT LOOKS GOOD ON YOU.

LAWSUIT

LOWER CLASS

NICE HOOTERS.

THANKS.

FLIRTING

CASUAL FLIRTING IS ACCEPTABLE, BUT YOU SHOULD AVOID THESE EXTREMES.

IT IS RUDE TO ACTIVELY ENCOURAGE FLIRTERS WHILE ON A DATE.

GOOD, GOOD. NOW DO THIS ONE.

IT IS RUDE TO NEGOTIATE IN FRONT OF YOUR DATE.

IF YOU'RE INTERESTED, I COULD BREAK IT OFF WITH HIM RIGHT NOW.

AND IT IS VERY RUDE TO ACT LIKE YOUR DATE DOESN'T EVEN EXIST.

FIVE MORE MINUTES AND YOU CAN JUST <u>FORGET</u> THE MOVIE.

HUSBAND REVENGE

HUSBANDS MAY ANNOY WIVES WITHOUT BEING RUDE IF THEY FOLLOW THESE TIME-TESTED METHODS.

CLICK

CHANGE CHANNELS QUICKLY AND CONSTANTLY AS IF YOU WILL NEVER STOP.

CLICK CLICK CLICK CLICK CLICK CLICK CLICK CLICK CLICK CLICK CLICK

BUY TOOLS FOR THINGS SHE DIDN'T EVEN KNOW YOU NEEDED A TOOL FOR.

I NEEDED IT TO DEMAGNETIZE THE RAIN GUTTERS.

BECOME UNUSUALLY ANIMATED AND ATTENTIVE IN THE PRESENCE OF ATTRACTIVE WOMEN.

KISSING AND TELLING

IT'S OKAY TO KISS AND TELL, AS LONG AS YOU OBSERVE SOME SIMPLE RULES OF TACT.

WAIT AWHILE. DON'T TELL RIGHT AWAY.

I'M SERIOUS, MONICA. IT WAS LIKE KISSING A SQUID...

A DESCRIPTION IS SUFFICIENT. THERE'S NO NEED TO RE-ENACT THE EVENT.

THEN ONE OF US STARTED KISSING LIKE THIS.

DON'T TELL YOUR UNATTACHED MALE FRIENDS. IT'S CRUEL.

I'M GLAD I HAVE A FRIEND WHO LISTENS TO MY ROMANCE STORIES IN ALL THEIR BORING DETAIL.

KNEE ROOM

WHEN A BIG UGLY MAN STEALS A WOMAN'S KNEE SPACE, THE WOMAN HAS THREE ALTERNATIVES.

AVOIDANCE AND THOUGHTS OF VIOLENCE

EXPLAIN THE SITUATION CLEARLY AND APPEAL TO HIS SENSE OF SOCIAL EQUITY. (NOT RECOMMENDED)

SHE WANTS ME. MY PLAN IS WORKING.

IMAGINE AN INVISIBLE LINE BETWEEN OUR SEATS...

ACCIDENTAL SODA SPILL

OOPS! SORRY! SOMEBODY BUMPED MY KNEE.

MEN HUGGING MEN

IN WESTERN CULTURES, WHEN HETEROSEXUAL MEN HUG THEY MUST OBSERVE CERTAIN CONVENTIONS.

KEEP THE NAUGHTY PARTS AT LEAST FOUR FEET AWAY.

DO NOT USE THE OPPORTUNITY TO REVEAL YOUR FEMININE SIDE.

DON'T LET ANYBODY SEE YOU GET THE HEEBIE-JEEBIES AFTERWARD.

POLITE TURN-DOWN LIES

PREGNANCY AND WEIGHT

PREGNANT WOMEN CAN BE SENSITIVE ABOUT WEIGHT GAIN. DO NOT MAKE THESE MISTAKES.

WHEN'S THE BABY DUE? TOMORROW?

IN SEVEN MONTHS.

AH, MUST BE TWINS, RIGHT?

NOPE.

WHEN YOU'RE "EATING FOR TWO" HAVE YOU CONSIDERED THAT THE BABY IS ABOUT THE SIZE OF A GOLF BALL?

PUBLIC DISPLAYS OF AFFECTION

SAYING NO TO A DANCE

IF AN UNDESIRABLE PERSON ASKS YOU TO DANCE, USE THESE METHODS TO POLITELY EXTRACT YOURSELF.

PRETEND YOU DON'T KNOW THE LANGUAGE.

MAY I HAVE THIS DANCE?

QUACK QUACK QUACK QUACK QUACK

S. Adams

SPILL YOUR DRINK ON HIS PANTS.

THIRD TIME TONIGHT. IT CAN'T BE A COINCIDENCE.

SPLASH

FIND A SACRIFICIAL DANCER TO TAKE YOUR PLACE.

SHARING YOUR DREAMS

DO NOT TELL PEOPLE WHAT ROLE THEY PLAYED IN YOUR DREAMS, NO MATTER HOW MEANINGLESS IT SEEMED TO YOU.

DILBERT, I HAD A FASCINATING DREAM ABOUT YOU LAST NIGHT.

I DREAMED IT WAS A BEAUTIFUL SUMMER EVENING. THE MOON WAS FULL...

YOU APPEARED AS A FIELD RODENT. I CRUSHED YOU WITH A BIG FLAT ROCK.

THANKS FOR TELLING ME.

S. Adams

STARING

IT IS IMPOLITE FOR A MAN TO GET CAUGHT STARING AT A WOMAN. MEN MUST USE THESE TRICKS TO AVOID DETECTION.

S. Adams

EXORCIST METHOD

USE REFLECTIVE SURFACES

CLEVER DECOY METHOD

WHERE DID YOU GET THAT NICE NECKLACE?

THREE "MOODS" OF THE MONTH

TO MEN, IT MAY SEEM THAT WOMEN HAVE THREE DISTINCT MOODS PER MONTH. THIS IS ONLY A MALE MYTH AND SHOULD NEVER BE MENTIONED.

S. Adams

"PRE"

STUPID BASTARD

"DURING"

I DIDN'T MEAN TO MENTION BLIMPS!! WE CAN TALK ABOUT SOMETHING ELSE!!

INSENSITIVE BASTARD.

"DENIAL"

YOU SEEMED A BIT MOODY YESTERDAY.

NO I WASN'T.

BASTARD

WIFE REVENGE

THE FOLLOWING ACTS ARE STILL PERMISSIBLE BUT THEY'VE BEEN ADDED TO THE WATCH LIST.

PUT YOUR COLD FEET ON HIM.

COOK LARGE QUANTITIES OF SOMETHING HIDEOUS AND MAKE IT CLEAR THAT YOU FEEL "VULNERABLE" TONIGHT.

IT'S OKAY IF YOU DON'T LIKE IT.

ASK HIM TO PICK UP SOME PERSONAL ITEMS AT THE STORE.

AFTER GOLF, WOULD YOU MIND STOPPING AT THE STORE?

S. Adams

LAUGHING AT TRAGEDY

IT IS NOT POLITE TO LAUGH AT THE MISFORTUNE OF OTHERS, UNLESS IT BECOMES A HEALTH RISK TO CONTAIN IT.

S. Adams

IT WAS TWO YEARS AGO THAT I LOST MY HUSBAND AT "JUNGLE SAFARI WORLD."

I SAID, "HONEY, PLEASE DON'T MOON THE CHEETAHS. THEY LOOK FAST."

DON'T LAUGH.

SOME PEOPLE THINK IT WAS "FUNNY."

LAUGHTER AS DEFLECTION

YOU MAY USE LAUGHTER AS A POLITE WAY TO DEFLECT UNWANTED INVITATIONS.

TRY A SMALL LAUGH FIRST.

I WAS THINKING MAYBE WE COULD GO TO A MOVIE.

HEH-HEH HEH

IF THE OFFENDER DOES NOT GET THE HINT, ESCALATE.

MAYBE SATURDAY?

HA HA HA HA HA

IF THIS TECHNIQUE DOES NOT PRODUCE RESULTS, QUIT BEFORE IT GETS UGLY.

I LIKE A WOMAN WHO CAN LAUGH EASILY.

HA-HA

BORING PEOPLE

BORES AT MEETINGS

THERE ARE THREE POLITE METHODS FOR DEALING WITH BORES AT MEETINGS.

FEEL FREE TO HAVE SIDE CONVERSATIONS IF YOU NEITHER FEAR NOR RESPECT THE PERSON SPEAKING.

SO THEN I SAID TO BOB...

BLAH BLAH

BLAH BLAH

S. Adams

BRING CRUNCHY FOOD AND TRY TO DROWN OUT THE SPEAKER.

THEN I SAID... CRUNCH

CRUNCH CRUNCH

CRUNCH

CRUNCH CRUNCH

CRUNCH CRUNCH

INTERRUPT FREQUENTLY SO YOU CAN USE UP THE MEETING TIME WITH YOUR OWN LONG-WINDED STORIES.

THAT REMINDS ME OF A STORY...

MMPH

BORING OTHER PEOPLE

IF YOU ARE BORING AND DON'T KNOW IT, USE THESE VISUAL CUES TO KNOW WHEN YOUR STORY HAS GONE ON TOO LONG.

STAGE ONE OF BOREDOM IS CHARACTERIZED BY SHRINKING PUPILS AND A ZOMBIE-LIKE STIFFNESS.

...SO I TRIED THE MATH COPROCESSOR SOCKET AND...

STAGE TWO OF BOREDOM IS CHARACTERIZED BY THE EYES ROLLING BACK IN THE HEAD AND A LOSS OF BALANCE.

...SO I SAID "WHO BURNED THESE EPROMS IN ANYWAY?"

IF YOU GET TO STAGE THREE, YOU MIGHT AS WELL JUST GO AHEAD AND FINISH YOUR STORY.

...AND THAT WASN'T EVEN THE INTERESTING PART!

S. Adams

DEALING WITH BORES

IN THE OLD DAYS, BEFORE TELEVISION, BORES WERE TOLERATED BECAUSE THERE WAS NOTHING BETTER TO DO. BUT IN THESE BUSY TIMES IT IS NECESSARY TO POLITELY DISMISS THEM.

SHOO!

... SO THEN I THOUGHT, WHY NOT EAT AN APPLE? SO, BELIEVE IT OR NOT, THAT'S JUST WHAT I DID. THEN I THOUGHT...

WAIT! STOP!

S. Adams

NO OFFENSE, BUT YOU'RE BORING ME TO DEATH. IF YOU CAN'T COME UP WITH SOMETHING INTEREST-ING THEN I'LL HAVE TO ASK YOU TO SHUT UP.

GEE, I'M SORRY.

NOPE. NOT INTERESTING. I HAVE TO ASK YOU TO SHUT UP NOW.

DISCOURAGING A SERIAL TALKER

A "SERIAL TALKER" IS A PERSON WHO CAN TALK CONSTANTLY AND FOREVER WITHOUT PAUSING FOR TOPIC SHIFTS. YOU MUST DISCOURAGE THEM.

YAK — YAK — YAK — YAK YAK YAK

S. Adams

SUBTLE HINTS DO NOT WORK.

NOTICE THE SERIAL TALKER'S TRANCE STATE

YAK YAK YAK

NEWS

HIDING WILL NOT WORK.

THEY WILL FOLLOW YOU ANYWHERE

YAK YAK YAK YAK YAK

THE ONLY KNOWN SOLUTION IS TO PLUG THE HOLE.

DANG! THIS ONE KNOWS SIGN LANGAUGE!

YAK YAK YAK

IF ONE CHILD IN THE FAMILY HAS NO RESEMBLANCE TO THE OTHERS, IT'S BEST TO LEAVE THE TOPIC ALONE.

THESE ARE MY SONS, JOHNNY, JACK AND BIFF.

IT CAN BE EMBARRASSING TO SINGLE OUT A FAMILY MEMBER WHO LOOKS "DIFFERENT."

JOHNNY AND JACK LOOK JUST LIKE YOU... BUT BIFF... GEE, THAT'S UNUSUAL...

DON'T MAKE IT WORSE BY SPECULATING.

WAIT A MINUTE... IS YOUR GARBAGEMAN GUS SIMPSON?

BABYSITTING

IF FRIENDS IMPOSE ON YOU TO BABYSIT IT IS WITHIN YOUR RIGHTS TO CONVERT THE CHILD TO A NEW RELIGION.

THANKS FOR AGREEING TO BABYSIT, DOGBERT.

SHOO! HAVE FUN.

DAVE, YOUR PARENTS ARE HEATHENS. LET ME TEACH YOU THE WAYS OF DOGBERTISM.

LATER

THANKS, DOGBERT. WE WON'T IMPOSE ON YOU LIKE THAT AGAIN.

I WOULDN'T THINK SO.

BRAGGING ABOUT YOUR KID

EMBARRASSING STORIES

YOUR MOTHER HAS A LIFETIME RIGHT TO TELL EMBARRASSING STORIES ABOUT YOU.

DID I EVER TELL YOU THE CUTE STORY ABOUT JEFFREY'S FIRST VISIT TO THE ZOO?

S. Adams

HA HA! WELL, JEFFREY WAS JUST REACHING PUBERTY, AND STILL CONFUSED ABOUT A LOT OF THINGS ...

NO NO PLEASE !!!

LATER

... AND TO THIS DAY HE'S STILL BANNED FROM THE MONKEY CAGE AREA.

GRANDPARENTS AND GRANDCHILDREN

GRANDPARENTS MAY SEEK REVENGE ON THEIR CHILDREN BY HOW THEY TREAT THE GRANDCHILDREN.

GRANDPARENTS MAY ONE-UP THEIR CHILDREN'S GIFTS.

G.I. JOE

KEYS TO YOUR AMPHIBIOUS ASSAULT VEHICLE.

GRANDPARENTS MAY TELL STORIES TO REMOVE ANY SHRED OF RESPECT THE CHILDREN MIGHT HAVE FOR THEIR PARENTS.

YOUR DAD TRIED OUT FOR THE GIRL'S BASKETBALL TEAM, BUT HE DIDN'T MAKE IT.

GRANDPARENTS MAY SPOIL THE GRANDCHILDREN WITH LOW LEVELS OF DISCIPLINE.

I'M NAKED AND I'M GOING TO HITCH-HIKE TO NORWAY.

HAVE FUN, DEAR.

MOTHERS VERSUS FATHERS

IT IS NOT POLITE TO INSULT A PERSON'S MOTHER. HOWEVER, FATHERS ARE FAIR GAME.

YOUR FATHER IS SO DUMB HE DRIVES HIS CAR BACKWARD TO REFILL THE GAS TANK.

HE'S THE ONLY PERSON WHO EVER BOUGHT AN INDOOR KITE.

HE WAITED YEARS TO HAVE CHILDREN BECAUSE HE THOUGHT IT WAS WRONG TO SLEEP WITH A MARRIED WOMAN.

HEY! IS THAT AN INSULT TO MY MOTHER?

S. Adams

FUNERAL ETIQUETTE

NEVER USE THE OPPORTUNITY OF SOMEBODY'S DEATH TO PLAY A PRACTICAL JOKE, UNLESS IT'S A REALLY GOOD ONE LIKE ONE OF THESE.

R.I.P.

S. Adams

THE "BORED TO DEATH" GAG

THAT WAS A GOOD STORY, BARRY, BUT I THINK ALICE WAS A BIT BORED.

THE "BREATHING" GAG

HE'S BREATHING!

THE "SCRATCHING TO GET OUT" GAG.

SCRATCH SCRATCH

DOGBERT'S CLUES FOR THE CLUELESS

TELEPHONE

ANSWERING THE PHONE

TO BE A TELEPHONE RECEPTIONIST, LEARN THE THREE MAJOR BEHAVIORS WHICH ARE CONSIDERED GOOD MANNERS.

SPEAK LIKE A ZOMBIE ON A COFFEE BUZZ AND HIT "HOLD."

HELLOUNITEDCONGLOMERATE IHATEMYJOBSOPLEASEHOLD.

CLICK

ACT LIKE TAKING A MESSAGE WOULD BE A MAJOR BOTHER.

SIGH. THAT WOULD REQUIRE PAPER... AND A WRITING THING... I COULD CHECK AROUND...

ACT LIKE A TEMP WORKER WHO WAS TRANSPORTED INTO THE BUILDING IN A SEALED BAG.

I DON'T KNOW WHO DOES THAT... I DON'T KNOW OUR ADDRESS... I DON'T KNOW WHAT PRODUCTS WE MAKE.

S.Adams

TAKING CALLS

YOU CAN MAKE PEOPLE FEEL INSIGNIFICANT BY ANSWERING YOUR PHONE WHILE THEY'RE IN YOUR OFFICE.

S.Adams

...AND SO, IT'S CLEAR THAT WE HAVE THREE OPTIONS...

RRRING

EXCUSE ME, THIS IS PROBABLY SOMETHING MORE IMPORTANT THAN YOU. FEEL FREE TO STARE OUT MY WINDOW.

UH...

RRRING

NO, NO PROBLEM. THIS IS A GOOD TIME TO TALK...

VOICE MAIL ETIQUETTE

VOICE MAIL IS A GOOD WAY TO POLITELY BLOW OFF PEOPLE YOU'D RATHER NOT SPEAK TO.

S.Adams

LEAVE A MESSAGE THAT INSTILLS HOPELESSNESS AND DESPAIR IN THE CALLER.

...I'M NOT HERE. IF THIS IS AN EMERGENCY CALL JACKIE...HA HA... AS IF SHE ANSWERS HER PHONE. BEEP

LEAVE CONFUSING AUDIO MENU CHOICES.

...BUT IF YOU HAVE TYPE "AB" NEGATIVE BLOOD AND YOU'RE TALL BUT NOT BLONDE PRESS THE SQUARE ROOT OF 42 ON YOUR KEYPAD...

RETURN YOUR VOICE MAIL CALLS DURING LUNCH TO AVOID GETTING A LIVE PERSON. THEN LEAVE ILLOGICAL ANSWERS TO THEIR QUESTIONS.

THE ANSWER TO YOUR QUESTION IS "TROUT." I HOPE THAT HELPS.

WHEN TO CALL

PEOPLE DON'T SIT AROUND WAITING FOR YOUR CALL; THEY'RE <u>ALWAYS</u> BUSY. YOU MUST LEARN WHICH ACTIVITIES ARE BEST TO INTERRUPT.

S. Adams

DON'T CALL DURING DINNER— PEOPLE ARE HARD TO UNDERSTAND.

BONT CHLOL BLURING MINNER, MLUTHEAD !!

DON'T CALL FROM 9 PM TO 11 PM UNLESS YOU WANT EVERYBODY'S PERSONAL LIFE TO BE JUST LIKE YOURS.

SO, WHAT ARE YOU DOING?

THE BEST TIME TO CALL IS AT 3 AM. THAT WAY THE CALLEE THINKS IT'S AN EMERGENCY AND GIVES YOU FULL ATTENTION.

SO, WHAT ARE YOU DOING?

HOME-MADE GIFTS

YOU CAN MAKE POLITE PEOPLE UNHAPPY BY GIVING THEM HOME-MADE GIFTS TO DECORATE THEIR HOMES.

IMPOSE YOUR HOBBIES ON OTHER PEOPLE'S HOMES.

I TRIED TO CAPTURE THE MOST COLORFUL MOMENT IN DUCK HUNTING... AND IT'S ALL YOURS.

PERSONALIZE THE GIFT TO MAKE IT HARD TO GIVE AWAY.

IT'S YOUR HOUSE, MADE ENTIRELY FROM PASTA!

SOLVE YOUR RECYCLING PROBLEM AND ANNOY YOUR FRIENDS AT THE SAME TIME.

ALL YOU NEED IS A LAMP SHADE!

BOTTLES

SELECTIVE INVITATIONS

USE THESE TRICKS TO
AVOID INVITING AN
UNPOPULAR CO-WORKER
TO YOUR PARTY.

THE FLAWED DIRECTIONS TRICK

IS THIS MAP RIGHT?
DO YOU REALLY LIVE
IN NEW ZEALAND?

EMPHASIZE THE POSITIVE

CONGRATULATIONS!
YOU MADE THE LIST
OF ALTERNATES. IF
SOMEBODY DIES DURING
THE PARTY WE'LL CALL
YOU!

YES!

SPECIALLY TRAINED DOGS CAN
CUT THE UNDESIRABLES FROM
THE HERD.

I HOPE YOU
ALL CAN MAKE
IT.

GIFTS FOR PARTIES

FOR SOME STRANGE REASON IT IS EXPECTED THAT GUESTS BRING GIFTS TO PARTIES.

GENERALLY, A HOST WILL KNOW IF YOUR GIFT IS SOMETHING YOU FOUND IN YOUR GLOVE COMPARTMENT.

A BREATH MINT STUCK TO A MAP. GEE.

AVOID GIFTS WHICH REQUIRE ANY SPECIAL MAINTENANCE.

LOOK, HONEY, IT'S A BALD EAGLE.

HOLD ONTO YOUR GIFT UNTIL YOU'RE SURE THE PARTY IS WORTH IT.

NOT SO FAST. I'D LIKE TO LOOK AROUND FIRST.

S.Adams

ENTERTAINING GUESTS

GUESTS ARE ANNOYING. THEY EAT YOUR FOOD AND MAKE YOU MISS GOOD TELEVISION SHOWS. USE THESE TRICKS TO AVOID REPEAT VISITS.

WE USED TO JUST THROW AWAY THE SOAP BARS WHEN THEY GOT SMALL.

HAVE YOU HEARD THE DIGITALLY REMASTERED "TINY TIM" CLASSICS?

WHICH WAY TO YOUR BATHROOM?

I DON'T HAVE ONE.

BAD GIFTS

DO NOT SIT PASSIVELY AND ACT LIKE YOU ENJOY A POORLY THOUGHT OUT GIFT.

BE HONEST

SHODDY CRAFTSMANSHIP, HAPHAZARD DESIGN... YEAH, I THINK IT'S TIME TO CONSIDER ADOPTION.

SOME GIFTS — LIKE TUBE SOCKS AND A PAPER WEIGHT — CAN BE COMBINED TO MAKE ONE GOOD GIFT.

SOMETIMES YOU CAN FIND A WAY TO GET ENJOYMENT FROM PURELY PRACTICAL GIFTS.

THANKS FOR THE GRAVY BOAT, SWEETHEART.

MISCELLANEOUS ETIQUETTE

PEER PRESSURE

PEER PRESSURE IS WHAT YOU DO TO PEOPLE WHO ARE NOT, IN YOUR OPINION, PEERS.

YOU CAN CREATE YOUR OWN FUN WITH PEER PRESSURE.

I'LL BET YOU'RE NOT SOBER ENOUGH TO DISASSEMBLE YOUR CAR IN THE DRIVEWAY.

Panel 3:

IT MAY BE NECESSARY TO GLAMORIZE AN ACTIVITY TO GET OTHERS TO JOIN IN.

IT MAKES YOU COUGH AND STINK AND DIE. TRY IT!

WHAT HAVE I GOT TO LOSE?

Panel 4:

THERE IS NO LOGICAL LIMIT TO THE FUN YOU CAN HAVE WITH PEER PRESSURE.

DON'T BE A WUSS. YOU CAN PULL OUT BEFORE IT HARDENS IF YOU GET SCARED.

WET CEMENT

PET ETIQUETTE

THANK YOU NOTES

SOME PEOPLE FOLLOW AN ANCIENT PRACTICE OF WRITING THANK YOU NOTES. THEY MUST BE STOPPED.

WELL-BRED PEOPLE WITH TINY NOSES WRITE PERSONAL NOTES TO THANK PEOPLE FOR ANYTHING.

Thank you for selling those tires to me. I shall cherish them always.

THE WELL-BRED PEOPLE WITH TINY NOSES MUST BE LOCATED AND STOPPED.

SHE'S HERE.

EVENTUALLY WE CAN RID THE WORLD OF THIS OUT-DATED AND INEFFICIENT PRACTICE, THUS REDUCING THE EXPECTATIONS ON THE REST OF US.

VACATION PICTURES

REMEMBER THESE TIPS WHEN LOOKING AT PEOPLE'S BORING VACATION PICTURES.

S. Adams

DON'T GUESS WHAT THE PICTURE IS SUPPOSED TO BE.

HEY, IT'S A WALRUS... WEARING YOUR BEACH HAT... OH...

SARCASM IS OKAY BECAUSE IT WILL GO COMPLETELY UNNOTICED.

DO YOU HAVE ANY MORE PICTURES OF FLORIDA CLOUDS? THEY'RE SO DIFFERENT!

ISN'T IT AMAZING?

DON'T QUESTION A PERSON'S PHOTOGRAPHIC TALENT.

I DON'T THINK A PHOTO OF THE MONA LISA IS ART IN ITSELF.

DIDN'T YOU NOTICE I USED BLACK AND WHITE FILM?

RECOGNIZING FINE ART

YOU WOULDN'T KNOW FINE ART IF IT BACKED OVER YOUR HEAD WITH A TRUCK. USE THESE CLUES TO KNOW WHEN YOU SEE IT.

IT'S "FINE ART" IF THE MALE PERFORMERS WEAR TIGHTS.

I ADORE SHAKESPEARE, AND I LOVE THE BALLET.

THERE'S A PATTERN HERE.

IT'S "FINE ART" WHEN PEOPLE WITH EATING DISORDERS DON COSTUMES AND SHOUT AT EACH OTHER IN ITALIAN.

AND OPERA ALWAYS MAKES ME WEEP.

WELL, IT BORES ME TOO, BUT YOU DON'T SEE ME CRYING ABOUT IT.

PAINTINGS OF "FINE ART" ARE THOSE DONE BY ARTISTS WHO ARE EITHER INSANE OR AT LEAST VERY SENSITIVE.

THE ARTIST HANGED HIMSELF BECAUSE OF A BAD HAIRCUT.

FINE ART.

S. Adams

CLEANING FOR COMPANY

SOMETIMES YOU GET SO ACCUSTOMED TO YOUR OWN FILTH THAT YOU DON'T SEE IT. USE THESE CLUES TO TELL WHEN YOU SHOULD TIDY UP FOR GUESTS.

CLUE #1: THE SHOWER HEAD IS SHORTER THAN IT USED TO BE AND THERE ARE STALACTITES.

CLUE #2: IT BECOMES INCREASINGLY DIFFICULT TO TELL THE BABY FROM THE CAT.

CLUE #3: THE PARAKEET DIES AND YOU ACCIDENT- ALLY BURY IT IN THE DINING ROOM.

BORROWING STUFF

IF YOU FIND SOMEBODY NICE ENOUGH TO LEND HIS POSSESSIONS, GET ALL YOU CAN BEFORE SOMEBODY ELSE DOES.

I NOTICED YOU WEREN'T USING YOUR FAMILY SO I DECIDED TO BORROW THEM.

HEY, IT FEELS LIKE YOU'RE NOT EVEN USING A LOT OF THESE INTERNAL ORGANS.

I CAN'T BELIEVE THERE WAS SO MUCH GOOD STUFF LEFT.

FLAUNTING YOUR WEALTH

NO MATTER WHAT YOUR INCOME, THERE IS SOMEBODY POORER TO MAKE YOU FEEL SUPERIOR.

USE THESE TECHNIQUES TO RUB IT IN.

COMPLAIN ABOUT YOUR TAX BURDEN.

IF NOT FOR MY SIX HOMES, THE TAXES WOULD EAT ME ALIVE.

I WISH.

S. Adams

BRAG ABOUT YOUR FOOLISH CONSUMER HABITS.

I ONLY USE "SUPREME ULTRA UNLEADED" GAS. IT'S THE SAME AS "UNLEADED" BUT WITH A MUCH COOLER NAME.

COMPARE YOUR ASSETS, FEATURE BY FEATURE.

DOES THAT MODEL HAVE "PICTURE IN PICTURE"?

COLOR TV

SUFFERING FOOLS

USE THESE METHODS TO POLITELY ENDURE THE FOOLS IN YOUR LIFE.

TO KEEP FROM KILLING THEM, TRY READING AND HUMMING AS A DISTRACTION.

WHAT IF ALL THE PEOPLE ON WELFARE BECAME LAWYERS? PROBLEM SOLVED.

HMM HMM HMM

IT IS NOT YET POLITE TO USE ELECTRIC STUN GUNS ON FOOLS. HOWEVER, IF ENOUGH PEOPLE DO IT, IT BECOMES ACCEPTABLE BASED ON THE PRINCIPAL OF "COMMON USAGE."

YOUR BEST BET IS TO FIND A WAY TO TRAP ALL THE FOOLS IN ONE PLACE, THEN LEAVE.

BARGAINS

FLEA MARKET

S.Adams

OTHER RELIGIONS

NEVER DISCUSS RELIGION WITH THOSE WHO ARE SO IGNORANT THEY DON'T SUBSCRIBE TO YOUR BELIEFS.

NEVER MIX LOGIC AND RELIGION.

...BUT IF HE'S OMNIPOTENT AND HE CREATED ME, IT MUST BE HIS FAULT IF I SIN.

LET ME PUT IT THIS WAY: SHUT UP.

DON'T MAKE JOKES ABOUT GOD TO PEOPLE WHO ARE NERVOUS ABOUT RETRIBUTION.

I USED TO HEAR GOD'S VOICE ALL THE TIME. BUT I TALKED HIM INTO PLAYING "EASY LISTENING" MUSIC INSTEAD.

AND DID I MENTION NEVER TO MIX LOGIC AND RELIGION?

WHAT HAPPENS TO THE FOUR BILLION PEOPLE WHO DON'T KNOW THAT GOD LOVES ALL HIS CHILDREN?

ETERNAL HELL.

PUBLIC LAUNDRY ETIQUETTE

PUBLIC LAUNDRY FACILITIES HAVE SPECIAL RULES OF ETIQUETTE.

THERE IS NO DRESS CODE. YOU CAN WEAR ANYTHING THAT IS STILL CLEAN.

IF SOMEBODY LEAVES THEIR LAUNDRY IN THE WASHER THAT YOU WANT, YOU HAVE THE RIGHT TO SCULPT A LAUNDRY BUNNY WITH THEIR STUFF.

NO MATTER HOW BORED YOU GET, IT IS NOT ACCEPTABLE TO TALK THE NIGHT JANITOR INTO TAKING A DRYER RIDE.

IT'S ONLY TWENTY-FIVE CENTS!

SWEARING

POLITE SOCIETY IS ACCEPTING MORE AND MORE SWEARING. YOU MUST TRY HARDER IF YOU WISH TO SHOCK.

*%!!☆!

IN THE OLD DAYS, SWEARING WOULD EASILY SHOCK PEOPLE.

BULL FEATHERS

THESE DAYS THE TRADITIONAL SHOCKING WORDS ARE OVER-USED AND INEFFECTIVE.

AND IN THE WEATHER, IT LOOKS LIKE A *!@☆% DAY TOMORROW.

SO IN ORDER TO SHOCK SOME-ONE YOU MUST CHOOSE WORDS SO VILE THEY CAUSE PEOPLE AND THEIR PETS TO CATCH FIRE.

I THINK I MADE MY POINT.

AAAGH

THE OPEN ZIPPER

IT IS YOUR DUTY TO DISCREETLY INFORM A MAN IF HIS TROUSER ZIPPER IS DOWN. USE CUTE TERMS TO MINIMIZE THE EMBARRASSMENT.

EXCUSE ME, BUT YOU'RE "FLYING LOW."

WHAT?

LET'S SEE, UH...

MISTER ED IS LEAVING THE BARN?

THE SHUTTLE BAY DOOR IS OPEN?

WILLY'S GOING TO THE CIRCUS?

WHAT ARE YOU TALK-ING ABOUT?

IF THAT DOESN'T WORK, TRY GUIDED IMAGERY.

YOU ARE IN A HOTEL IN PARIS ... THE CURTAINS SHOULD BE CLOSED BUT INSTEAD YOU SEE THE EIFFEL TOWER OUTSIDE...

BAD HAIRPIECES

WHEN CONFRONTED WITH A BAD HAIRPIECE TRY TO AVOID THESE MISTAKES.

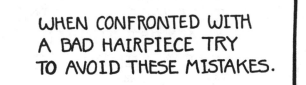

S. Adams

NO MATTER HOW TEMPTING, DO NOT SLAP IT OFF.

DON'T BE CONDESCENDING, UNLESS YOU DISGUISE IT AS SARCASM.

IT MUST BE TOUGH TO HAVE SO MUCH TESTOSTERONE COURSING THROUGH YOUR VEINS.

DO NOT BECOME OBSESSED BY THE HAIRPIECE AND STARE TRANSFIXED WHILE TALKING.

WHAT THE HECK IS HE THINKING?

I THINK SHE'S AROUSED.

IF YOU CAN'T SAY SOMETHING NICE...

IF YOU CAN'T SAY SOME-
THING NICE ABOUT A
PERSON THEN AT LEAST
SAY IT BEHIND HIS
BACK.

I ONCE HAD A DATE
THAT WAS SO BORING
I ALMOST JUMPED
OUT A WINDOW TO
GET AWAY.

S.Adams

BUT THEN I THOUGHT
HA! HE'S SO CLUELESS
I CAN HAVE FUN BY
MOCKING HIM IN FRONT
OF OTHER PEOPLE.

LUCKY FOR YOU
THAT YOU'RE
DATING ME
NOW.

FAKING SYMPATHY

BEING POLITE MEANS OFTEN HAVING TO PRETEND THAT YOU CARE ABOUT OTHER PEOPLE'S PROBLEMS.

S. Adams

SINCERE SOUNDING SYMPATHY ALWAYS USES MORE THAN ONE WORD.

... WE LOST THE FARM AND WE ALL HAVE METAL PLATES IN OUR HEADS.

BUMMER.

OTHER PEOPLE'S PROBLEMS ARE BORING. TRY DISGUISING YOUR YAWNS AS CRIES OF SYMPATHY.

HE CARES.

YAAARGH !!

TRY TO TOP THEIR STORY WITH TALES OF YOUR OWN WOE.

SO THEN I ...

I THINK I'M GETTING NEAR-SIGHTED IN ONE EYE.

DOGBERT'S CLUES FOR THE CLUELESS

DISABILITIES

DOGBERT'S CLUES FOR THE CLUELESS   109

DOGBERT'S CLUES FOR THE CLUELESS

CONSTRUCTIVE CRITICISM

CRITICISM IS OFTEN CONSTRUCTIVE BECAUSE IT MAKES YOU FEEL SUPERIOR WHEN YOU GIVE IT.

I WAS JUST NOTICING HOW UGLY YOU ARE COMPARED TO ME.

DIDN'T I SEE YOU IN THE MOVIE "MASK"?

HEY! I'M WITTIER THAN YOU TOO! MAN, I'M FEELING GOOD. THANKS!

DOGBERT'S CLUES FOR THE CLUELESS